Farmhouse cider
and scrumpy

Bob Bunker

Bossiney Books · Launceston

NDSMAN'S BOOKSHOP LTD.
Bromyard, Herefordshire, U.K.
Tel/Fax +44 (0)1885-483420

How to live to 120

I were brought up on cider
And I be hundred and two
But still that be nuthin' when you come to think
Me father and mother be still in the pink
And they were brought up on cider
Of the rare old Tavistock brew
And me granfer drinks quarts
For he's one of the sports
That were brought up on cider too.

First published 1999 by
Bossiney Books, Langore, Launceston, Cornwall PL15 8LD

© 1999 Bob Bunker

All rights reserved

ISBN 1-899383-16-6

Acknowledgements
The photograph on page 7 is reproduced courtesy of The Beaford
Photographic Archive. All other photographs, apart from the cover
(by Andrew Besley), were specially taken for this book by the publishers.
Cover design by Peter Bennett, St Ives.

The author and publishers would like to thank the following for their help
in the preparation of this book: Burrow Hill Cider, Countryman Cider and
Perry's Cider Mills.

Printed in Great Britain by R Booth (Troutbeck Press), Mabe, Cornwall

Traditional cider

Each year around 500 million litres (110 million gallons) of cider are drunk all over Britain. This isn't really surprising, as it's been known for hundreds, probably thousands, of years that the simple fermentation of sugars in apple juice produces an excellent liquor.

The large commercial cider-making companies account for over 98 per cent of the annual figure. The remainder, ciders full of character and never the same from season to season, is generated by small-scale farm cider makers, most of them in the West Country. Many of these provide cider as a side-line to their main crops – just like their predecessors did in the past.

In producing 'farmhouse cider', the small cider makers are continuing an art which until the 20th century was never written down – each generation learned the basic principles by watching and practising, and then they tried to improve on what had been done before them. Cider makers have always striven for the best, for their own perfect combination of fruit, equipment and special blending that results in a glorious golden liquid which works wonders on the palate.

Also known in Devon and Cornwall as 'scrumpy', farmhouse cider (or cyder) is made from the pure juice of apples specially bred for the purpose – eating apples are not at all suitable. Natural yeast is used and fermentation takes place under normal atmospheric conditions without the addition of artificial ingredients. The resulting cider is either still or has a light liveliness, and is usually clear – although it can also be slightly cloudy. But the real proof is in the drinking, and a visit to some of the many makers who open their doors to welcome visitors is very worthwhile. All have their own secrets, their own ways of getting the best – this book gives some of the clues as to how they, and their forebears, have achieved success.

Cider

The apple and its juice have been used in cooking and drink making for as long as history has been written. Cider apples were introduced to Britain in Celtic times, probably before the arrival of the Romans, while cider making is first recorded in 1205 in Norfolk. By 1300 it had spread to the whole of southern England. The popular drink eventually became a sort of currency for many years: high grade liquor, possibly strengthened with honey, was given to local authorities and landlords in payment of taxes and rents. In Devon, cider was made on a commercial scale and was transported by ship to ports along the coast to London, and even overseas.

During the Civil War, Charles I sent his son Charles (later Charles II) to the West Country to join the Royalist Army. When they were defeated in Cornwall, Charles fled with a small group to the Isles of Scilly, taking with them as part of their stores 30 hogsheads of cider (around 7250 litres/1600 gallons) from Werrington, near Launceston. Even at the age of 16, the young prince had his priorities right!

In 1697 Gerard observed in his *Herbal*: 'the servants drink for the most part no other drink than that which is made from apples'. Writing in Devon in 1720, T Cox says:

> the fruit trees are very plentiful especially apples, with which they make such great quantities of cider... The merchants, who go great voyages to sea, find it a very useful drink in their ships, and so buy up great store of it; for one ton of cider will go as far as three of beer and is found more wholesome in hot climates.

Opposite: Ripe cider apples in a Somerset orchard. Cider apples come in many colours and shapes, and the art of the cider maker lies in skilful blending of their differing flavours

Before it was discovered that lime juice prevented scurvy, just one wine glass of real cider a day given to crews on long journeys was enough to keep the disease away (James Cook chose to carry cider with him to Tahiti on the *Endeavour* in 1768). However, casks of cider for future sale and not for medicinal purposes were often broken into by sailors, and on arrival their contents were found to be diluted with water or were vinegary.

Early in the 18th century a form of colic was common among cider drinkers in Devon. People naturally put it down to something in the dry local cider and, hardly surprisingly, it soon became known as 'Devon colic'. But in areas where cider was made in the same way, such as Gloucester, Herefordshire and Worcester, there were no problems, and the mystery deepened.

After nearly seventeen years Dr George Baker, a Devonian, realised there were similarities with the colic suffered by workers in the lead mines, and he brought out a paper blaming lead in the cider industry for the Devon colic. Lead was indeed readily available, and was used as a sealant between stones on the mills and presses. More importantly, lead salts were often added to cider to give it a sweet taste, especially when it had started to go slightly vinegary! Eliminating the lead quickly got rid of the Devon colic, but by this stage cider's image had taken a nose dive. Its popularity declined and with it many cider-making skills and many of the best varieties of cider apples.

Things weren't helped by the Cider Truck Law which allowed up to a third of workers' wages to be paid in cider. This encouraged farmers to produce large quantities of poor quality, often adulterated cider. A small resurgence of interest came with the canals in the 19th century and the possibility of distributing to a wider population. But this was shortlived: wines were imported freely from abroad and the cost of replacing mills and presses was beyond the pocket of most small farm cider makers.

A few landlords installed new equipment which tenants could use, but by the end of the 19th century the industry was in disarray. Fortunately, there were still a few enthusiasts, including Mr R Neville Granville of Butleigh Court near Glastonbury. After completing a survey of cider making in 1893, he was struck by the 'utter lack of knowledge of the underlying principles of cider making' and 'the crudeness of the methods used in cider production on farms'. As a result, in 1903 the National Fruit and Cider Institute was set up and, with the forerunner to the Ministry of Agriculture, it investigated all aspects of cider.

Using the information gathered and their own expertise, large production companies – Bulmers, Gaymers, Whiteways and Coates – greatly expanded. Sadly, however, most of these have since disappeared or been absorbed by larger organisations. It is now the small makers of farmhouse cider in the West Country, with their professional skills and enormous enthusiasm, who are continuing to bring traditional cider and scrumpy to thousands of customers each year. Thanks to them the art of cider making will continue.

Farmworkers enjoying a traditional drinks break

Orchards and apples

The ideal place for an orchard is a sunny, sheltered field with good well-drained soil. But in the past the best positions were reserved for animals and for crops more important than cider. A single farm's cider needs were not large, so an orchard of up to twenty trees was planted in any available space, often in small fields that were difficult to plough or to clear of stones.

Today some traditional cider makers in the West Country continue to use some of these old orchards. Others have created much bigger areas for their fruit trees.

Cider apples

All apples can be grouped into four main categories based on their acid and tannin contents:

type of apple	category	acid	tannin
eating	sweet	low	low
sweet cider	bittersweet	low	high
sharp cider	bittersharp	high	high
cooking	sharp	high	low

Good cider apples, which have had 2-3000 years of breeding, have several distinct qualities. They are fibrous, like a sponge, which means that when they are pulped the juice is squeezed out cleanly and the solids can be discarded easily. Eating and cooking apples don't press as cleanly or give as clear a juice as the proper cider apple.

The juice contains a good supply of sugar for conversion to alcohol during the fermentation process (see page 23), but on the whole cider apples do not taste sweet. This is because of their high levels of tannin that have a bitter, drying effect on the palate. Tannin, which is also in red wine and tea, is responsible for the golden orange colour of the cider: a high tannin content is said to make a brighter and more stable drink.

Deliveries of apples (above) to the small producer Countryman
Cider and (below) to Burrow Hill Cider (also home to the
Somerset Cider Brandy Company)

Flavour, as opposed to sweetness, is found mainly in the skin. In cider apples the skin tends to be much thicker than in eating apples whose thinner skins are easier to bite through. Although eating apples have a good flavour, many are quite unsuitable for cider because when the sugar is fermented off such acids as do remain are unpleasant. The complex nature of cider apple juice makes it durable: it can go through all the processes over a long period and the flavour will still be intact at the end.

Varieties of cider apple

There are over 400 varieties of cider apple grown in Britain, and there are as many names, plus local variations, as there are varieties – their names often come from an apple's physical characteristics, such as Pig's Snout and Cider Lady's Fingers (put your finger tips together and hang them from your wrist, and you'll have some idea of what this apple looks like).

Only 5-10 of the varieties are considered suitable to make cider on their own. These are known as vintage apples and they have a depth of aroma and flavour that will enhance any drink, the most widely used being Kingston Black. In Devon and Cornwall, where a sweeter cider is preferred, Dabinett, Major, Yarlington Mill, Sweet Coppin and Sweet Alford are also popular. Most ciders, however, are made from a mixture of varieties.

Harvesting

Apple trees tend to have biennial traits, which means a good crop one year often leads to a poor one the next. Over the years cider makers learned to thin out blossom and young fruits in a good year to balance out unevenness in cropping. They also bred their cider apples to fit in with the farming calendar: the earliest varieties are not ready for pressing until the beginning of October, by which time most grain harvests have been gathered and animals are in winter quarters. (It also means that the blossom appears later in the year, and avoids the frost that can hit early flowering eating apples.)

As pressing has to fit round other things to be done on the farm, further varieties of cider apple were bred to be cropped in November, and a third batch in December – a few late varieties will still be hanging on the trees in sheltered spots in January, allowing pressing to spill over into the new year.

Cider apples are not normally picked. Instead, windfalls are gathered regularly and stored on a dry floor to avoid rotting. After about half the fruit has fallen, the rest can be shaken off the branches. Mild bruising does not affect the flavour, but bad or discoloured apples are thrown away.

Wassailing

There is always something to be done in the orchard throughout the year, be it pruning, which can start in August and finish the following March, or calling on the deities to give a hand with next year's crop. Traditionally, the ancient ritual of 'wassailing' takes place on the twelfth night after Christmas when the whole community gathers in their local orchard to ward off evil spirits.

First a small boy is sent up into the branches of a tree where he leaves a piece of toast soaked in cider (called 'basting'). The crowd then sings or shouts either:

> Here's to thee old apple tree
> Whence thou mayst bud and whence thou mayst blow!
> Hat's full! Caps full! Bushel, bushel sacks full,
> And my pockets full too! Huzza!

or:

> So well they might bloom, so well they might bear,
> That we may have apples and cider this year.
> Hats full! Caps full! Three bushels bagsful!
> Little heap under the stairs,
> Hip! Hip! Hooray!

The verse is repeated and after the third time a drink of cider is taken, some thrown on the tree and some on the ground. Afterwards the evil spirits are driven out with much noise from sticks, rattles and shotguns! The party then moves on to the next tree and the process begins again. This carries on until it's time to retire indoors for something to eat.

The colourful tradition continues each year on 17 January at the Butcher's Arms in Carhampton, Somerset. Toast is dipped into mulled cider in the wassail bucket which is then placed in the apple trees to ensure a good crop the following year.

Another form of wassailing happened at Christmas when poorer families carried round a maple wood bowl of cider, often warmed and spiced, and offered a drink at the richer houses in exchange for alms. In Truro in Cornwall, to keep this under control, only certain families were issued with licences to wassail.

A mixture of varieties in the silo, awaiting milling

Above: Apples can be moved and washed in a stream of water to the elevator which will then deliver them to the mill, or (see the photograph on the right) they can be fed from the silo by gravity with control from a Wellington boot! Faulty apples are removed on the way

Milling and pressing

Mixing all apple varieties together to make cider is usually a safe bet, as any anomalies in one variety will be evened out by the others. The more difficult choice of blending just two or three varieties will usually be based on experience gained over some years and will also depend on what is available in the orchard.

Cleanliness

Before any mechanical process takes place, all the equipment must be clean – at no time is the juice sterilised by heat (unlike beer or some wines). However, the natural organisms essential for successful cider making must not be killed.

Apple juice and cider stain almost any surface dark brown, nearly black. Sodium hypochlorite, which is used to keep swimming pools and drinking water clean, will bleach this off, but it will also leave a nasty flavour in any juice that comes into contact with it. So everything has to be rinsed with a sulphur solution that kills unwanted organisms and neutralises the flavour.

In the past sulphur candles were the accepted sterilisation method. They would be burnt in such a way that sulphur fumes rose into the bung hole of the casks or vats. This was sufficient to kill surface bacteria, but did not penetrate far into the wood, and so the action of these potentially harmful organisms was delayed rather than prevented.

Apple milling (or 'scratting')

Even when ripe, apples are large and hard fruits to press, and they must first be broken down. This not only allows the juice to be extracted more easily, but also encourages further 'maturing' by allowing enzymes in the apple to convert more of the starch into sugar – as much sugar in the juice as possible is needed for the fermentation stage.

The physical breaking down of the fruit is done by using a mill. The traditional granite mill or 'pound' had a circular trough, about 400 mm (15 inches) deep and 1.2-4.5 metres (4-15 feet) in diameter. An attached donkey or pony would walk round and round outside, rolling a millstone set on its edge into the trough. This pulverised the cider apples into a pulp, called 'pomace' or 'murc'. (Some millstones were smooth and others were grooved, as was the bottom of the trough, which caused the stone to roll unevenly or 'pound'.)

During the 19th century smaller mills were worked by hand or steam. These were called 'scratters' and were made with two wooden rollers inset with iron spikes above and two granite mill wheels below, all on horizontal axles. They speeded up the milling process, and were often mounted on a trailer and towed round the local farms on a shared or hired basis. In recent years, most farm cider makers have installed electrically-driven mills, with knife blades that rotate at high speed and grate the apples.

Pomace 'cheese'

The pulp or pomace has a porridge-like consistency and is brightly coloured with the apple skins. It's important that it does not have a long exposure to the air at this stage, otherwise oxidation will alter the flavour and darken the juice. (You can see the effect of oxidation when you slice an apple and leave it uncovered.)

The clean juice is separated from the crushed fruit, leaving as much solid matter behind as possible. For hundreds of years this was done by using the long straw left over from the season's grain crops as a filter. Layers of pomace were interspersed with matted layers of straw until a stack, or 'cheese', had been built. It was usually about 1 metre (3 ft) square and 1 metre high, and contained around 500 kg (half a ton) of apple. Each straw layer was folded up and over the next apple layer, thereby containing the solid matter as the juice was extracted by pressing.

In some places coarse mats of horse hair replaced straw. After pressing, the spent pomace could be shaken off the 'hairs' which were then ready to be re-used, although they were heavy and difficult to keep clean. As new man-made materials were invented, they were greatly welcomed. But because these are lighter and softer, the cheese can easily become flimsy. To make it more rigid, every layer is now built onto a rack. Each rack is made from ash wood slats laid in two layers at right angles to each other. A small gap between them helps to channel away the juice from the cheese during pressing.

At one time the cheese would be built up on a solid base under the press, with channels to drain the juice into buckets or straight into a cask. Today the cheese is built up in a trolley that has raised sides and just one outlet for the juice. There are usually two trolleys for each press so that while one cheese is being pressed another can be made.

Pomace from the mill is used to build a cheese at (left) Perry's Cider Mills and (opposite) at Countryman Cider

Great care must be taken when building the cheese so that the layers are aligned properly. Pomace is quite slushy and if it is not evenly distributed the next layer will settle at an angle. If this carries on up the cheese, the result can be the whole lot (half a tonne) slithering onto the floor – a messy predicament!

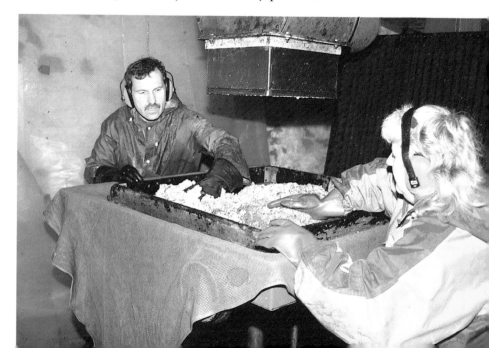

Pressing

As a general rule of thumb, 1 tonne of apples should yield 670 litres (148 gallons) of juice. Over the centuries improvements and modifications to presses were designed to reach this figure in the shortest possible time. Farmers making their own cider naturally looked to local materials and skills. When woodworkers and blacksmiths were on hand, the early presses relied on massive timber structures with long levers that would bring the maximum sustained pressure onto the cheese. Where local stone was available, large blocks were lowered onto the top of the press to help the process.

In the 19th century metal castings and gearing made the task easier, but it still took a day to press a single cheese – and even then there was an unacceptable amount of juice left in it. The pressed pomace was broken down, mixed with water and then pressed again. The second pressing was weaker than the first, and was often used to make 'small cider' for the labourers in the fields during the year. This was considered part (it could be up to a third) of their wages until the end of the century.

The stronger, first pressing was kept for use by the farmer and his family and was also sent out for sale. Its extra strength helped preserve the cider from bacterial infections and so gave it a longer life.

As presses became more sophisticated, smaller farmers in Devon were unable to afford one of their own. Landlords often installed a large press on their estate and tenant farmers brought their apples and pressed them. Part of the juice was retained by the landlord as payment for use of the press.

With the introduction of the hydraulic press in the early part of the 20th century, the process was at last shortened considerably: a cheese weighing around 500 kg (half a ton) can now be pressed in 20-30 minutes. The extra pressure has also improved the extraction rate, and 'small cider' is rarely made.

Cider apple juice

The taste of a cider apple straight from a tree is, on the whole, not something most people find attractive. On the other hand, the pure juice coming off the press seems to have undergone a magical transformation. It is sweet, almost syrupy, with a background of rich scented flavours – and the tannin leaves the mouth feeling dry. There is always a tendency to have another drink, but beware! Cider apple juice is very rich and can inconvenience you greatly if you over-indulge. It is said that older members of cider-making teams encouraged inexperienced ones to go on drinking the juice. At the very least they would have a painful stomach for several days.

Unfermented juice straight from the press was often sold during the 19th century as 'cider from the pound's mouth'. It was bought by cider makers who would then complete the cider-making process to their own requirements.

While cider apple juice is not usually kept for drinking (juice for this purpose is generally a blend of eating and cooking apples), some cider makers retain a small amount to add to the final product in order to restart a small fermentation in the bottle or cask. This produces a light natural gassing, called 'petillance'.

Spent pomace

After pressing, about half the weight of the apples will be in the form of juice, sometimes called 'murc', 'marc' or 'must', and half will consist of solids – the fibrous flesh, peel, core and pips (called 'spent pomace') caught in the straw or cloths. After being thrown out with the straw or shaken from cloths, the spent pomace must be used within one or two days or it will become vinegary. It is traditionally given as extra winter feed to farm animals: it doesn't have much nutritional value, but they seem to like it as an option to silage at this time of the year.

Above: The freshly milled pomace

Below: Folding the cloth around each layer of the cheese is a job carried out with great accuracy and speed. The noise of the mill makes it safer to use ear protectors

Above: The completed cheese is manoeuvred in its trolley precisely beneath the press. Below: Juice oozes out and is collected from an outlet in the trolley behind the cheese. This kind of press is no longer available, so the old ones are carefully maintained

Above: Removing the cloths after the pressing. Notice how compressed the layers of the cheese now are

Below: The spent pomace is tossed off the cloth onto a farm trailer, and will be taken away and fed to cattle. In many countries farmers distil a product variously called eau de vie, schnapps and brandy from a liquid collected by sealing up the spent pomace into barrels for six months or so

Fermentation

Yeast

When the juice or must is transferred from the press to the fermenting vats or casks, it comes into contact with the air. This is important, as the yeast cells need oxygen to breed. They then live by consuming the sugar in the juice, the by-products being alcohol and carbon dioxide. This simply is the fermentation process. The aim is to keep the alcohol in the juice to make cider, and to allow the carbon dioxide to escape.

At this stage the must contains a considerable amount of small solid matter. It is run into a scrupulously clean vat, and after two or three days the yeast activity is vigorous enough for the gas to lift some of the finer solids to the surface. If the vat has been filled to the top with juice, the frothy mixture of solids and gases will be ejected from the bung hole and spill out to where it can be washed away. Alternatively, it can be skimmed from the surface with a jug or spatula, a process known as 'keeving'.

As much solid matter as possible is removed, after which all outlets from the vat are sealed to avoid air and its potentially harmful bacteria coming into contact with the surface of the juice. An airlock is then fitted at the top of the vat which allows the gas to escape rather than build up pressure inside.

Another precaution to prevent contamination is to leave a small gap over the juice. This will soon be filled naturally with carbon dioxide with a slight pressure which will form another barrier to any air leaking into the vat and coming into contact with the juice.

Temperature

The best temperature for any sort of fermentation is between 15°C and 30°C. However when cider is being made, in the later part of the year, the air temperature is below this range. This is actually beneficial, as the delicate flavours and aromas will stay in the juice rather than evaporate into the atmosphere along with the carbon dioxide. The ideal is a slow fermention over two or three months.

In order to thrive, yeast needs a very small amount of protein as well as sugar. If it is lacking, then a long spell of cold weather will virtually stop the fermentation process and it can be extremely difficult to restart it. Farmhouse cider is traditionally fermented in outbuildings where there are no ways of regulating temperature. This means that frosty spells can halt fermentation, while milder weather increases it. In the past, to overcome the problems brought on with the severe cold, it was found that essential protein in the form of a small piece of meat suspended in the vat was enough to keep the fermentation active. This naturally led to stories of rats and other oddities being added to the juice! These days a small amount of ammonium thiosulphate does the job in a more hygienic way.

It is a pleasant diversion on a calm morning in mid-winter to go into the fermenting room and listen to the vessels 'talking' to you. The gas bubbles out from the air locks, and if you place an ear on a vat you can hear a low murmuring inside as the bubbles are formed and rise to the surface. The whole liquid mass circulates due to convection currents and gas production, and this movement can be seen if the top hatch is removed for a quick look. But if you do this, be careful not to be overcome by the carbon dioxide fumes!

Racking

As fermentation continues, there is less and less food for the yeast, and the cells start to die and settle to the bottom of the vat. There they soon break up and produce substances that can damage the flavour and clarity of the cider. To stop this happening, the cider is 'racked' into a clean storage vat, leaving the

Right: This big barrel can hold over 2700 litres (600 gallons) of cider – the juice from 4 tonnes of apples

Below: rows of barrels waiting for the autumn pressing period at Perry's

yeast at the bottom of the original one. This precipitation is aided by cold weather – chilling the juice slows the yeast activity and will cause most to drop to the vat bottom.

Racking is normally carried out just before all the sugar has been fully used, and after a cool spell is an opportune time. It can be done by siphoning or pumping the liquid carefully from the vat top to disturb the yeast as little as possible.

Storage

The storage vat is filled to the top and sealed so that the cider cannot come into contact with the air. If it is still cloudy, it may be racked a second or even a third time.

From here onwards the cider is very vulnerable to spoilage by acetic bacteria. These are present in the air and on poorly cleaned equipment, and they live by converting alcohol to acetic acid. They will take only a short time to increase the acidity of the stored cider, eventually turning it into vinegar. Casks and vats made from wood are particularly at risk: apart from being difficult to clean, they are slightly porous and allow air to enter. It is for these reasons that a tiny amount of sugar is left in the cider in the final racking, or it may be added on a weekly basis if small amounts of cider for drinking are to be drawn off over a prolonged period of time. (This will also increase the cider's alcohol level!)

The few cells of living yeast feed slowly on the sugar. They produce carbon dioxide which cannot now escape through an airlock. It therefore builds up a pressure in the vat which will prevent any air coming in and so will keep the cider in good condition. It also gives the drink a pleasant sparkle when the time comes for sampling. Of course if you leave too much sugar in the juice, the pressure can damage the container and cause all your efforts to erupt onto the floor!

In the past there was great difficulty keeping large wooden vessels free of air-borne infection once they had been opened. All the cider was run into smaller barrels which were topped up to the bung. Casks were then used in rotation. When they became half full there was a danger of the top staves shrinking, and letting gas out and air in. To get round this problem, the casks were kept wet on the outside with dampened sacking. This also kept the cider cool in the summer.

Maturation

The flavour of cider matures as it ages, especially in the first nine months, due to the chemical changes taking place in the juice. But cider is perfectly drinkable at all ages, from very fresh to two or three years, as long as attention is paid to its storage. If kept in wooden casks or vats, the juice may darken in colour over time and take up some of the flavours of the wood.

When they were readily available, imported wooden barrels previously containing brandy, rum and sherry were used for storing cider. The cider then took up some of the flavours and aromas of its predecessors. Sadly today such casks are rare and available only at enormous expense.

Blending

This is the fun bit! If a small quantity of cider has been made, it's more than likely that all the apples have already been mixed together and so there's nothing to do except enjoy it. On the other hand, if larger quantities are involved, the chances are that the earlier storage vessels had different selections of apples from the later ones. The results will therefore be ciders with varying acidity, colour, alcohol and tannin contents. Acidity and tannin affect the taste, so if some samples have unnatural highs or lows it may be possible to even out the extremes and arrive at a balance by blending two or more ciders together.

For traditional cider makers it is usually a subjective choice affected by practical considerations. It is these choices made by individuals from an infinite number of combinations that distinguishes their cider from others.

Bottling

Bottling farm cider gives it a much longer life if it has to travel. Cider makers often add a tiny amount of sugar before sealing so that the cider has a pleasant amount of gassing when poured

Most of the farmhouse cider makers who open to the public offer tastings and sell a wide variety of ciders and cider products

out. The quantity of sugar is critical: too much means too much fermentation and pressure... and burst bottles.

If filtering is available, it is possible to remove the yeast, which results in a clear, still cider. This is not quite as good a method for storing, as there is no layer of carbon dioxide in the space below the seal to prevent infection from unwanted organisms.

A superior style of cider can be arrived at by using champagne methods of bottling and maturing. The process involves a lot of space, equipment and attention over many months, and also requires strong bottles and high-grade corks specifically manufactured for champagne.

Twice as much sugar is added as in the first method mentioned here. The bottles are sealed and the corks wired or clamped into place. They are then placed on their side for the secondary fermentation stage which takes place at a low temperature during six to twelve months. At the end of fermentation each bottle is tilted neck-down and is turned very slightly every day so that over time all the deposit moves down the glass and settles on the cork. This sediment is 'disgorged' by plunging the neck into a freezing solution, undoing the wire and allowing the gas pressure to force out the cork along with it. The trick is to lose as little as possible of the liquid. The bottle must be topped up and recorked very swiftly. The result is a very fine, but expensive cider.

Dry and sweet cider

The strength of cider is determined by using a standard winemaker's hydrometer to get a specific gravity reading. This is around 1050 for fresh juice from the press and should then ferment out to 1000 or below for the final product (equivalent to about 6.5% 'alcohol by volume' – ABV).

When all the sugar has been used up, the end cider will be a traditional dry one. This is what most West Country people drank in the early days. But with the growth of trade with London and elsewhere, the demand for a sweeter cider increased. It was traditionally made by stopping the fermentation when about half the sugar had been consumed (not a very exact science) and racking two or three times. It is less alcoholic than dry cider, as only part of the sugar is converted to alcohol. In turn this means it is less able to resist infections and needs to be drunk as early as possible.

In the days of wooden cask cider, the killing off of the remaining yeast was achieved by 'candling' or 'matching'. In *The Climate of the South of Devon*, Thomas Shapter says:

a small quantity of juice (say a gallon) is then drawn off into an empty cask, and while a sulphur match is being burnt within the bunghole, the juice is agitated round the sides of the cask, the remainder is then added: this process is repeated in a fresh cask, as often as it shows a tendency to ferment. In cold or still weather two matchings are sufficient, but when the weather is hot and windy it may require to be done four or five times.

Shapter continues:

at first [the cider] is very sweet and raw, and tastes of apple, predisposing those who drink it to griping pains and diarrhoea, but at the end of three or four months becomes a palatable and wholesome liquor.

Cider brandy

Cider brandy has been made in Spain and in France, mainly Brittany and more famously the Calvados area of Normandy, for hundreds of years. The Somerset Cider Brandy Company has the only commercial licence in the UK to distil cider into cider brandy. It is made by the careful distillation of fully fermented cider to concentrate the alcohol and flavours into a product with an alcohol content of around 42% ABV. The distillate, which is almost colourless, is matured in oak casks for at least three years during which time the brandy matures, becomes smoother, and picks up some of the tannins in the oak.

The tower stills used are complex, expensive and require a high degree of skill and experience. The final product also needs special expertise in tasting and blending. And Customs and Excise apply strict controls to all stages of production.

Cider drinks

Cider fruit cup (makes 3 glasses)

    570 ml (1 pint) tonic water
    570 ml (1 pint) medium farmhouse cider
    40 g ($1^{1}/_{2}$ oz) concentrated orange juice, chilled
    12 ice cubes
    sprigs of mint
    orange slices

Chill the tonic, cider and orange juice concentrate. Make the orange juice up to 570 ml (1 pint) with cold water and add the tonic, cider and ice cubes. Mix well and serve in glasses decorated with sprigs of mint and orange slices.

Summer celebration cup

    225 g (8 oz) small strawberries
    3 tablespoons orange liqueur
    1 orange
    570 ml (1 pint) medium dry farmhouse cider
    570 ml (1 pint) soda water
    ice cubes

Wash and hull the strawberries and place them in a bowl. Add the orange liqueur and the juice of the orange. Cover and leave to stand overnight. Next day add the cider, soda water and ice cubes. Serve in glasses.

Sangria (makes 16 glasses)

    2 lemons and 2 oranges, sliced
    2 apples, cored and sliced
    12 ice cubes
    2 litres (4 pints) sweet farmhouse cider
    2 bottles inexpensive red wine
    1 glass brandy
    2 to 4 tablespoons caster sugar, according to your taste

Chill the wine and cider well. Then place all the ingredients together in a very large mixing bowl and stir thoroughly. Serve at once in wine glasses.

Cider/gin cocktail

.1 litre (2 pints) dry farmhouse cider, chilled
rind of 1 lemon, thinly peeled
1 wine glass of gin

Make sure the cider is chilled. Place the lemon rind in a large jug, pour the gin over it and leave to stand for 30 minutes. Then add the cider, stir and serve at once.

Mulled cider

1 litre (2 pints) medium farmhouse cider
mixture of spices made up into muslin bag (8 cloves,
    8 allspice, small stick cinnamon)
sugar to taste

Heat the cider in a saucepan, with the bag of spices suspended in it, until it is just simmering. Allow to simmer for 5 minutes, then remove the spices. Add sugar to taste and drink while it is still hot. Additional ingredients may be added, such as ginger spice, orange juice, brandy or whisky.

Also note: cider makes an excellent substitute for wine in most (if not all!) food recipes calling for the addition of such liquor.

Customs regulations

If you decide to make your own cider, please remember that anyone selling over 7000 litres of cider must be registered with Customs and Excise who have their own definition of cider (agreed with the National Association of Cider Makers) and a list of permitted ingredients.

For customs purposes apple juice becomes cider, and therefore liable to duty, when there is a 1.2% ABV. Any cider stronger than 8.5% ABV is called a 'made-wine' and is liable to duty at a much higher rate. Basic farm cider is unlikely to be more than 6.5% ABV unless extra sugar is added to the juice. Customs & Excise Notice 162 gives all the necessary information and is readily available from their advice centres.